Baby Booming America Back Again

Norah Wilson
Baby Booming America Back Again

—

Published by - Spines
ISBN: 979-8-89691-190-6

History is recorded in books, documents, and films—written, spoken, and remembered across time. Baby Booming America Back Again: Roe v. Wade Overturned adds its voice to these records, presenting facts, historical perspectives, and insights as they are known today.

The author does not claim to control the past, predict the future, or alter the truth. The names and events mentioned remain as they exist in public record, shared with the intent of education and discussion. This book does not seek to defame, slander, or misrepresent any individual or institution.

Additionally, this book contains discussions of abortion and religious viewpoints, which may be emotionally challenging for some readers. Discretion is advised.

While every effort has been made to ensure accuracy, the author and publisher make no guarantees regarding the completeness or absolute correctness of the information provided. Readers are encouraged to explore multiple sources and draw their own conclusions.

The author assumes no responsibility for how the content is received, interpreted, or used.

Baby Booming America Back Again

Roe Vs. Wade Overturned

Norah Wilson

Disclaimer:

American history, the times of life known to be once lived. History remembered and recorded in Films, documents and in books written by renowned Authors displayed in volumes upon the shelves in Universities, Colleges, Schools, Libraries and in our American homes all across the USA; BABY BOOMING AMERICA BACK AGAIN ROE VS. WADE OVERTURNED joins those authors who with this disclaimer share the awesome truths be it as it is known by our history books, and with spiritual enlightenment share the way things are now and with this disclaimer sharing the appearance of things to become in the near future. With this disclaimer, this book simply echoes and repeats bits, tidbits and pieces of whatever, however, whenever it happens at the end of a days end.

This is disclaiming the Author has no control over the things of yesteryear, or how it comes back around in another time or place in the future. The names of the people mentioned in this book have not been changed or altered any more than what was done in writings sitting on shelves years ago and has not been done by this author. This book is intended to be among other professional educational documents sources of one's choice. This is a disclaimer from having any personal point of view as the Author other than what has been written countless times before by history books or biblically.

This is a disclaimer from any discord any place or thing that may have a different view of things, religion or any other

BABY BOOMING AMERICA BACK AGAIN ROE VS. WADE OVERTURNED

IAMTHEVOICEINTHEBOOK

NORAH WILSON

A MESSAGE FROM THE AUTHOR

THE RIGHTS OF THE USA TO BEAR CHILDREN

Everyone has the right to self-control and to remain abstinent.

If you lose self-control, you give up your right to a probable, predestined conception!

One encounter with a male's sperm can—and is willed to—impregnate one egg!

Women have the maternal right to bear children.

If your baby's father cannot afford prenatal care, Care will be provided to you by the state.

Let's all understand our rights to **BABY-BOOMING AMERICA BACK AGAIN.**

ROE V. WADE OVERTURNED!

Testimonials

Baby Booming America Back Again... Roe vs Wade Overturned is a phenomenal, educational and informational book that all American women need to read! This amazing book has chilling information all throughout that I was completely unaware of that shocked me! Good

book, good,
good book!

-Anonymously, Indiana

Baby Booming America, Back Again...Roe Vs Wade Overturned....

This audiobook and book had me blown away this is so much information that has been spoke, not only informational, but spiritual. Being born in the 1980s this book really showed me not only about our history, but how abortions is really hurting our nations. As a bible believer this book open my eye to much more of what the spirit is trying to say to us through this author Norah Wilson. Baby Booming America Back Again... Roe vs Wade overturned is a must read. I rate this Audiobook and Book a 10!

- Taisha Cannon, Indianapolis, Indiana

Baby Booming America, Back Again...Roe Vs Wade Overturned...

I just loved how this audiobook and book makes you understand what's really going on In the world about how Women, lives was just monopolized in the 1940's Until today.

How can an individual change your perception of life to make you kill someone That later on in life makes you think of them, after you start having babies for your family you start having mental health issues that your husband doesn't even know you had an Abortion or miss carriage by either a ex or a rape baby? America as men doesn't and Will never understand to carry an unwanted child. So for someone to try and tell you what you can do with your body is so B.S just knowing as an individual women speaking outside the box. I will rate this audiobook and book a 10!

-Kalencia Kirkland, Indianapolis, Indiana

Baby Booming America, Back Again.... Roe Vs Wade overturned...

This audible book was very profound, strong, and formative. As I listened from the beginning to the end, I found myself in a few pages of the book, from being in the baby booming era to being raised in the church. Author Norah Wilson's book was so deep it even brought out the hidden things to THE LIGHT. The nation has been deceived, and the SPIRIT is speaking. The truth and information in this book had not only enlightened me but touched me in so many ways. Norah Wilson this book will change the world one page at a time! I rate this Audiobook and Book a 10!

Yolanda Parker, Indianapolis, IN

BABY BOOMING AMERICA BACK AGAIN...ROE VS. WADE OVERTURNED AUDIOBOOK AND BOOK is nothing short of a 2025 chiller! While listening to the audiobook, suddenly, I felt I was back in-history class or sitting in church; but no teacher or preacher told or had this effect on me... at one point I was moved to tears. I am a man, 34 years old, I didn't know anything about all of this. I realize and I can't help repeating myself here; this audiobook gives me chills! This audio and book tells of something bigger; it opened up something that to me was hidden and it's not over, it's a snowball effect this audiobook is a

MOVEMENT within itself! It's ready to expose the monster; swept underneath the carpet of Churches for years too long and now suddenly this Narrator is exposing this truth about a "monster" now ready to rear its ugly multiple heads. I'm shocked to learn the truth that 70% of the unliving of babies and birth control were done by the best of all people, "The Christians!" This narrator's smooth voice cuts deep into the truth that is just plain shocking to me; as a man, I'm not ever going to be the same after listening to this audiobook, what a spiritual awakening... BABY BOOMING AMERICA BACK AGAIN ROE VS. WADE OVERTURNED audiobook and book has opened up my understanding eye to see one person done so much bad for so many people.(the blind leading the blind and all falling into the ditch) This book and audiobook taught me the past repeats itself and with a vengeance; wow, what a spiritual awaking effect on me. I believe every child should be taught with this book being part of the history books. This Narrator makes it plain to understand how one woman's wrath, pain and torment turned into a public vengeance; a WAR THAT UNLIVED millions upon millions of U.S.A. BABIES IN THE WOMB AND THE SHOCK TO FACE THE FACT THAT WE REALLY ARE AN ENDANGERED SPECIES; A WAR THREATENING OUR NEAR FUTURE BY 70% OF CHRISTIANS. This audiobook and book are not what you may think it is to be, it's much much more than that what meets the eye, don't judge this audiobook or book by its cover or title. Listen as I did to this audiobook to be educated, parents need to be educated to be able to educate their children, and this audiobook, I believe beyond a shadow of doubt, will educate you. This audiobook and book is podcast material! I hope this book becomes a part two; this Narrator educated me more than ever; left me with labelling this audiobook and book with a shock factor, a warning and not for the faint of heart! This excellent narrator's voice lifts off the pages written in ink; skillfully etching and melting me with her smooth voice that articulates right into my secret part of my soul! I must rate this anointed Professor Norah Wilson, Author of her book, and Narrator in her audiobook; but first I must say I love this Author and her audiobook and book, and I now give a FIVE STAR RATING to this Narrator and her powerfully narrated educational audiobook and book, BABY BOOMING AMERICA BACK AGAIN ROE VS, WADE OVERTURNED! *****

M. J. Greenwood, Indiana

Contents

Prelude

To everything, there is a season and a time to every purpose under heaven: A time to be born, and a time to die; a time to plant, and a time to pluck up that which is planted; a time to kill, and a time to heal; a time to break down, and a time to build up; a time to weep, and a time to laugh; a time to mourn, and a time to dance; a time to rend, and a time to sew; a time to keep silence and a time to speak; a time to love, and a time to hate; a time of war, and a time of peace.

What profit hath he that worketh in that wherein he labored? All is vanity, saith the preacher. I have seen the travail, which the Divine Will of Light made the dark angel Lucifer: ruler over one end of the kingdom to the other. Lucifer is the Lord God who transformed himself as an angel of light, a deceiver of Adam, and now deceiving this world. It is he, along with the sons of Lucifer, known from old as "The Sons of God," who deceived from their beginning and hath blinded the minds of the sons of men to be exercised in it.

He hath made everything beautiful (vain) in his time: this beauty is not only vain but also empty and of pride that comes before deception. Also, he hath set this deception in their heart, the lust of his eyes, lust of his flesh, and the pride of life, so that no man can find out the work that the Lord God Lucifer of this world maketh as a curse of a cursed spirit from the beginning to the end unless man's eyes become spiritually opened (Ecclesiastes 3:11).

I know that whatsoever the Lord God Lucifer doeth (is "instinct" by the Will of the Light that made and gives Lucifer his power), it shall be forever; nothing can be put to it, nor anything taken from it. The Lord God Lucifer of this world, the ruler once over all in heaven but was cast down and doeth it in earth, that unfaithful men should bow down, worship, and fear before him. But we know fear is not of the Will of the Light of Truth! (Ecclesiastes 3:14).

A separation of the just is made by the Will of Light; this Will is Divine (permanent), Positive without darkness, and the Divine Will is Truth. Hell is a void for and of the lost, soulless spirits of darkness. That which hath been is now, and that which is to be hath already been, and the Lord God Lucifer of this world required that which is past (Ecclesiastes 3:15).

And moreover, I saw under the sun the place of judgment, that wickedness was there, and the place of righteousness, that iniquity was there (Ecclesiastes 3:16). I said in mine heart, the Lord God Lucifer of this world shall judge the righteous and the wicked, just as the Lord God Lucifer was named and given his rule over all the spirits, dark and of light, for there is a time there for every purpose and for every work concerning the estate of the sons of men, that the Lord God Lucifer might manifest them, and that they might see that they themselves become as beasts.

Only the eyes of the just understand that it is impossible to be deceived when you are chosen by the Light! For that which befalleth the sons of men is because of his disobedience to the honoring of his own Father and Mother... and disobedience is as the sin of witchcraft; to know good and not doing good is sin!

Who knoweth the spirit of man that goeth upward, and the spirit of the beast that goeth downward to the earth? Wherefore you may perceive that there is nothing better than that a man should rejoice in his own works, for that is his portion: for who shall bring him to see what shall be after him?

But there is one question I will ask of you, reader: do you know there is a difference between the sons of men (Adam and Eve) and the sons of the Lord God Lucifer who were destroyed in the flood of Noah? What does this have to do with anything? The sons of the Lord God Lucifer are among us, along with the strange daughters of men; this world was made for the Lord God Lucifer and his fallen angels of darkness! Hell has enlarged itself.

There are three things that will cause the wrath of the Lord God Lucifer upon the children of disobedience:

1. The lustful eye between a man and the strange woman.
2. The fornications and spiritual adultery between those that are not spiritually joined by the

Divine Will. (If your spirits are not joined, you just have a law of lust with your body)
3. The debauchery of the reproduction organs in birth control and mistreatment of children conceived. If any one of his fatherless children as much as cry out unto him, he will revenge them; it will be better for a millstone to be hanged around your neck and sling the anchor into the deepest parts of the sea and be drowned than to offend one of these little ones.

Woe unto the world because of offenses! For it must needs be that offenses come, but woe to that man by whom the offense cometh! Take heed that ye despise not one of these little ones; for I say unto you, that in heaven their spirit doth always behold the face of the truth.

The love of money, the lust of your eyes, and your pride in life have cost the lives of over 64 billion conceptions since Roe vs. Wade; when will the people see that the blind cannot lead the blind without falling into the pit?

Listen, there is a sound in the streets, weeping and gnashing of teeth...

To everything, There is a reason...An eye...For an eye...A cry for... Mama!

The King James Bible, a book composed of 66 smaller books, is respectfully referred to as 39 Old and 27 New Testaments. Ecclesiastes, book number 21, has 12 chapters or 12 little books of its own. My opening statement in this introduction quotes the third chapter among the 12 chapters from The Book of Ecclesiastes.

Beginning with the first verse, let's honor this passage

and take note of the second and third words: "everything." Everything means all is included, and nothing is excluded. Every person, place, and thing, being all matter that occupies space, is encompassed by this word.

The word "season" is often associated with the changes throughout the year, namely the four seasons: spring, summer, fall, and winter. In the Northern Hemisphere, spring begins on March 1, summer on June 1, autumn on September 1, and winter on December 1. Conversely, in the Southern Hemisphere, spring begins on September 1, summer on December 1, autumn on March 1, and winter on June 1.

While there are no official allocations for the four seasons, they are generally understood to coincide with the equinoxes and solstices that occur with the sun. A solstice is when the Earth's axis is most tilted toward or away from the sun, creating a time of distress. However, the seasonal change also brings solace to the atmosphere.

There is a season to give comfort or consolation to the soundlessness of nature, impressing and solacing her. As we explore the concept of seasons, we come to understand that not only is there a season for everything, but everything is seasonal. Summer has passed, and fall has come to America. The crops have been destroyed, and a famine has befallen the land. Americans are nearly extinct, depopulated by the war on the fetus. This is the season and time of winter. Crops are not planted in the soil during wintertime nor in the barren or aged females. We must look forward to springtime when new seeds can be planted in the fertile wombs of our American females and stop the maternal war in the U.S.A.

“BABY BOOMING AMERICA BACK AGAIN!”
(Roe Vs. Wade Overturned)

There Is A Season And A Time For War

What is war. A state or period of fighting; armed conflict between different nations or states, or diverse groups within a nation or State. It is a struggle of hostility between opposing forces or for a particular end.

There are diverse types of wars, including:

- **Civil War:** a public, courteous, or social conflict within a nation or State.
- **Nuclear War**: atomic warfare using nuclear weaponry.
- **Criminal War**: an action conducted during the conduct of a war that violates accepted international rules of war.
- **Revolutionary War:** a war of independence, such as the American Revolutionary War.
- **Marital War:** a declaration of war on one's spouse, including infidelity and divorce.

- **Biological War:** also known as germ warfare, the use of biological toxins or infectious agents such as bacteria, viruses, insects, and fungi with the intent to kill, harm, or incapacitate humans, animals, or plants as an act of war. Biological weapons are living organisms or replicating entities.
- **Korean War:** a war fought between North Korea and South Korea.

War on humanity refers to certain acts that are purposefully committed by a state or on behalf of a state as part of a widespread or methodical policy. These acts are typically directed against civilians in times of war or peace and are considered severe breaches of human rights. They differ from war crimes because they are not isolated acts committed by individual soldiers but are acts committed in furtherance of a state or organizational policy.

The first prosecution for crimes against humanity took place at the Nuremberg trials. Following the Holocaust, a global standard of human rights was articulated in the Universal Declaration of Human Rights in 1948. Political groups or states that violate or incite violation of human rights norms, as found in the Declaration, are an expression of the political pathologies associated with crimes against humanity.

War against humanity refers to specific crimes committed in the context of a large-scale attack targeting civilians, regardless of their nationality. These crimes include murder, torture, sexual violence, enslavement, persecution, enforced disappearance, and more.

Birth control is a war against the conception of humanity; abortion is a war against life, destroying the future generation of humanity. Pro-choice is premeditated murder; abortion is the homicide of the conception of the unborn. All forms of birth control, other than self-control, are committing a premeditated act against life, which is "prenatalcide."

Abortion is murdering the innocent, defenseless unborn while they are in a developing, unable-bodied, and handicapped state within the womb, at any time before birth, while still guarded by the mother's maternal protection. Abortion is rendering abuse and neglect to the unborn in any stage of life within the womb, which is the highest degree of "prenatalcide" and a spiritual debauchery.

A Time To Lose, Break Down, Weep & Mourn

Before the war, Germany, America, and the rest of the world were experiencing the Great Depression. The economy was in an unbelievably bad state, with unemployment at an all-time high and massive inflation causing money to lose its value.

The Great Depression was the worst economic downturn in the history of the industrialized world, lasting from the stock market crash of 1929 to 1939. On Thursday, October 24, 1929, as nervous investors began selling overpriced shares in masse, the stock market crash that some had feared finally occurred, marking a record 12.9 million shares traded that day, known as "Black Thursday."

Five days later, on Tuesday, October 29, 1929, the Dow Jones Industrial Average (DJIA) fell 12%, an event known as "Black Friday." Another wave of panic swept Wall Street, with 16 million shares traded and 12.5 million shares ultimately becoming worthless. Investors who had bought stocks "on margin" (with borrowed money) were wiped out completely.

The population of 121,767,000 Americans, forced to buy on credit, fell into debt, and the number of foreclosures and repossessions climbed steadily. The global adherence to the gold standard, which linked countries around the world in fixed currency exchange, helped spread economic woes from the United States throughout the world, especially in Europe.

Matters continued to deteriorate over the next three years. By 1930, 4 million Americans looking for work could not find it; that number had risen to 6 million in 1931. In 1932, with the country mired in the depths of the Great Depression and 15 million people unemployed, Franklin D. Roosevelt won an overwhelming victory in the presidential election.

By March 4, 1933, every U.S. state had ordered all remaining banks to close at the end of the day, marking a low point in the economic crisis.

There Is A Time To Cast Away That Which Is Planted

Meanwhile, the country's industrial production had dropped by half. Bread lines, soup kitchens, and rising numbers of homeless people became increasingly common in America's towns and cities.

Farmers couldn't afford to harvest their crops and were forced to leave them rotting in the fields while people elsewhere starved. In 1930, severe droughts in the Southern Plains brought high winds and dust from Texas to Nebraska, killing people, livestock, and crops. This period, known as "The Dust Bowl," inspired a mass migration of people from farmland to cities in search of work.

In the fall of 1930, the first of four waves of banking panic began, as large numbers of investors lost confidence in the solvency of their banks and demanded deposits in cash. This forced banks to liquidate loans in order to supplement their insufficient cash reserves on hand. Bank runs swept the United States again in the spring and fall of 1931 and the fall of 1932. By early 1933, thousands of banks had closed their doors.

A Time to Refrain from Embracing

The 1940 United States Census, the sixteenth census conducted since 1790, listed 134 million individuals enumerated that year. The index and images of population schedules provided a snapshot of the inhabitants of the United States at that time.

On September 12, 1940, the Hercules Munitions Plant in Succasunna-Kenvil, New Jersey, exploded, killing 55 people. Just four days later, on September 16, 1940, President Franklin D. Roosevelt signed the Selective Training and Service Act of 1940 into law, creating the first peacetime draft in U.S. history.

The first year of the 1940's was marked by war-related news. More than 50 nations around the world were engaged in conflict, with over 100 million soldiers deployed.

A Time To Weep, Mourn, Hate, Kill & Die

World War 2 began in 1939. It was the deadliest and most destructive war in history.

On September 1, 1939 (September 2, 1945) Hitler invaded Poland. It drove Great Britain and France to declare war on Germany, marking the beginning of World War 2. Over the next six years, the conflict would take more lives and destroy more land and property around the globe than any previous war.

Actually, in late 1939, the Nazis began the "Operation T4." It was the first mass killings of Germans and Austrians with disabilities, most by large-scale poison gas operations. This program alone resulted in the murder of an estimated 275,000 persons by the war's end.

Is there a difference between "war, killing, and death?" Can there be a war without killing and death?

Research shows the number of fatalities:

- **Civilian Deaths:** 45,000,000

- **Battle Deaths:** 15,000,000
- **Battle Wounded:** 25,000,000

An estimated total of 70-85 million people perished. It was about 3% of the total global population, which was around 2.3 billion estimated in 1940. Deaths directly caused by the war, including military and civilian fatalities, are estimated at 50-56 million, with an additional estimated 19-28 million deaths from war-related disease and famine.

Military deaths from all causes totaled 21-25 million, including deaths in captivity of about 5 million prisoners of war. More than half of the total number of casualties are accounted for by the deaths of the Republic of China and the Soviet Union. The Japanese government puts its casualties due to the war at 3.1 million.

By far, the biggest event for Americans in 1941 was the Japanese attack on Pearl Harbor on December 7, 1941, a day that would indeed, as FDR said, live in infamy. On May 24, the British battle-cruiser HMS Hood was sunk by the Bismarck during the Battle of Denmark Strait; the Royal Navy sunk the Bismarck three days later.

From June 22 to December 5, Operation Barbarossa, an Axis invasion of the Soviet Union, took place. The plan was to conquer the western Soviet Union and repopulate it with Germans, and in the process, the German armies captured some five million troops and starved or otherwise killed 3.3 million prisoners of war. Despite the horrific bloodshed, the operation failed.

The Nazis began a prolonged military blockade known as the Siege of Leningrad, which would not end until 1944. In the Babi Yar Massacre, Nazis killed over 33,000 Jews from

Kyiv in a ravine. The killing would continue for months and involve at least 100,000 people.

On April 9, 1942, at least 72,000 American and Filipino prisoners of war began a forced march by the Japanese. It was 63 miles from the southern tip of the Bataan Peninsula to Camp O'Donnell in the Philippines. An estimated 7,000-10,000 soldiers died along the way in what became known as the Bataan Death March.

On July 13, the first printed T-shirt worn in a photograph appeared on the cover of Life magazine. A man brandished an Air Corps Gunnery School Logo.

On April 30, 1945, Adolf Hitler and his wife Eva Braun committed suicide by cyanide and pistol. It was in an underground bunker under his headquarters in Berlin.

A Time Of Laughter, To Dance, To Sow Peace

On September 2, 1945, U.S. General Douglas MacArthur accepted Japan's formal surrender aboard the U.S. battleship Missouri. It was anchored in Tokyo Bay along with a flotilla of more than 250 Allied warships. This is how the Second World War ended.

A Time Of Love; To Plant, To Reap, Be Born!

On July 14, 1946, Dr. Spock's "The Common Book of Baby and Child Care" was published. It came just in time for the start of the post-war Baby Boom. Baby Boomers, often shortened to boomers, are the demographic cohort following the Silent Generation and preceding Generation X. Generation X is often defined as people born from 1946 to 1964. The U.S. population in 1950 was 150,398,453. In 1952, it rose to 152,941,7, showing a Growth Rate of 1.56%

The United States ended 1951 with a population of 153,970,000 people, which represents an increase of 2,099,000 people compared to 1950. The United States is a country with an exceptionally low population density, with 16 people per square km, and it was in position 2nd in a ranking of density population in 1951.

In comparison to the population of 130,884,000 in 1939, the United States ended 1956 with a population of

168,078,000 people, which represents an increase of 3,020,000 people compared to 1955.

That's a population boom if you go back to the year 1776 with a population of 2.5 million!

However, the population continued to boom. By 1964, the population grew to 191.9 million. This boom was a spike in birth rates after World War 2.

In the United States, around 3.4 million babies were born in 1946, more than ever before in United States history. This trend continued, with 3 to 4 million babies being born each year from 1946 to 1964.

By then, there were 76.4 million "baby boomers" in the United States. They made up almost 40% of the nation's population. Of the 76 million baby boomers born, nearly 11 million had died by 2012, leaving some 65.2 million survivors. According to the US Census Bureau, US boomers will remain the second-largest population group in 2022, comprised of 69.6 million people ages 58 to 76.

In December 1945, The United Nations Children's Fund (UNICEF) was founded in New York City.

The landmark holiday movie "It's a Wonderful Life" had its premiere; it opened to mixed reviews. Las Vegas began its transformation into the gambling capital of the U.S. with the opening of the Flamingo Hotel.

In 1947, Polaroid cameras were introduced. It was just in time for all those baby shots! The year ended not before World War 11 fighter pilot Chuck Yeager broke the sound barrier for the first time, flying in a Bell X-1 experimental aircraft.

Because every conception impact, good and bad, was to take place. Boomers have been categorized by their importance in the world, and this world does involve them. Career advancements from A to Z, from Astrologists to Zoology, from becoming the first humans to land on the surface of the moon.

The baby boomers were the first generation for which television became a central part of their lives.

Boomers were exposed to constant advertisements depicting the lifestyles of the richest, most famous Americans with whom they compare themselves.

A Time To Gather Stones Together & Build-Up

The sheer size of the baby-boom generation, some 75 million, magnified its impact on society. The growth of families led to a migration from cities to suburbs in the postwar years, prompting a building boom in housing, schools, and shopping malls.

Baby boomers value relationships. As they grew up, there was a growing belief in the value of spending time with family and friends. The boomers are goal-centric, self-assured, and are resourceful.

They also have destructive tendencies like selfishness, arrogance, and ruthlessness that can result in outright despotism or factional strife. During a baby boomer's midlife, they often reevaluate everything that has something to do with their personal life.

The core values of Baby Boomers include optimism, team orientation, personal gratification, health and wellness, personal growth, youthfulness, work, and involvement.

When a workplace environment supports their values, Baby Boomers are more satisfied with their jobs.

During the 1960's, the baby boomer's economic influence continued. As teenagers, the boomers dumped approximately 20 billion dollars into the U.S. economy every year.

Clothing, food, and recorded music were popular items, and businesses were more than happy to meet consumers' demands.

A Time To Be Silent, Break Down & Cast Away!

There is nothing new under the sun; what comes around has existed in another place or form. World War 2 was the deadliest military conflict in history; an estimated total of 70-85 million people perished, or about 3% of the 2.3 billion estimated people on Earth in 1940.

There is a time of peace to be celebrated with barbequing ribs, roasting hot dogs, toasting marshmallows bubbling over, torched by the flames of an open-air campfire. Americans were living the American dream, drinking Kool-Aid, lemonade, ice cream, popsicles, and homemade deep-dish apple pie. The baby boomers had never lived through the depression or seen death in war, but life is not always merry and certainly not a bowl of cherries, and it's not always good to get what we want without counting up the cost. Americans, like spoiled teenagers partying and free-loving, were unaware another war was coming on the horizon!

September 1969 was just an explosion of sexual revolution, as the Time Magazine cover states! Free love movement, but nothing is free; everything comes with a price. Freedom is just another word for nothing left to lose, but the baby boomers took a stand in the free love Era.

Gay Americans were protesting for their rights as well as far back in 1924. The birth of the modern gay rights movement in the United States was conceived from the uprising that broke out on June 28, 1969, when angry gay bar patrons decided the policemen had pushed them too far.

Harry Hay was considered the founder of the gay rights movement; It wasn't until 1969 that the movement gained momentum.

1969 was just one year in history that 76.4 million baby boomers lived; the future of 11 million baby boomers would die before the year 2012, but all in all in 76.4 million baby boomers that were born between 1946 and 1964, just one birth in 64 million was belonging to this one female infant. This passionate story of one dilemma after another caused havoc in the life of Norma Leah Nelson, who lived for 69 years.

One baby out of 76.4 million persuaded and seduced the government of the U.S. to pass a law legalizing women to premeditate and commit more than 69 estimated million predatorial deaths; this number is an estimation because so many abortions were committed behind closed doors, illegally in a way that is contrary to or forbidden by law.

This female grew up lawless yet was empowered by the State to make a law to commit prenatalcide of nearly 64 million lives that would depopulate a world lost today in an unmarked life forbidden to the right to live!

September 22, 1947, just another baby boomer, born in

Simmesport, southern State of Louisiana. This baby girl named Norma Leah Nelson was wrapped in a blanket while sleeping and was placed in the crook of the skinny arms of her frightened teenage, dysfunctional, unhappy, drug-addicted mother.

Norma's father was Olin Julius Nelson, a World War 2 veteran and a television repairman from Texas. In a tumultuous relationship that her father deserted, only returning a year later to separate from them permanently.

Who can say what Norma's mother felt about her baby? Her mother did not abort her unborn child. Norma's mother had her demons, that was for sure, but she kept her child and whatever life-life-threatening and fated against them. Norma knew her teenage, dysfunctional, unhappy, drug-addicted mother wanted her enough to keep her in her life. Still, Norma and her brother grew up impoverished and neglected as their mother's verbal and physical abuse was added to the trauma.

Norma was ten years old when she was in legal trouble and was sent to Mount St. Michael School for Girls. After poor behavior, she was transferred to the Gainesville School for Girls, which she called "the happiest time of her childhood."

She lived there off and on until she turned fifteen years old. Upon her release, her mother sent her to live with an older cousin, who she stated repeatedly sexually assaulted her until her mother brought her home.

On June 17, 1964, Norma married Elwood "Woody" McCorvey, moved to California, and soon became pregnant. After her husband became physically abusive, she returned to Dallas and got a divorce. She gave birth to a daughter, Melissa McCorvey, in 1965.

Soon after, Norma came out as a lesbian to her mother, who, with her father's help, had her declared an unfit parent and then adopted Melissa. The LGBTQ community in Oak Lawn took Norma in and became her family.

Norma battled problems with depression and alcohol and substance abuse and had a series of jobs and relationships. During relative stability, she worked as a respiratory therapist and had a steady girlfriend until a short liaison with a man left McCorvey pregnant and alone.

Norma also lost her job; her employer had a policy that pregnancy was grounds for termination for unmarried female employees. She placed the child for adoption at birth. She continued her transient life with forays into selling and using illicit drugs, playing billiards in bars for money, and working for a traveling carnival. Late in 1969, while at the carnival, Norma learned she was pregnant. She returned to Dallas and the LGBTQ community that had helped her in the past.

She did not want to go through pregnancy again and had a challenging time finding employment outside of bartending. Her options, however, were limited. At the time, Texas law prohibited abortion in all cases except when medically necessary to save a woman's life.

Norma could not afford the travel expenses to New York and California, the only states where abortion was legal, so she sought out how to get a sage abortion illegal without success.

She even claimed that her pregnancy was a result of rape,

which she admitted later was a lie, with the hope that an exception to the law might be made. A physician put Norma in contact with attorney Henry McCluskey, Jr., who arranged the adoption.

He put her in contact with Linda Coffee, an attorney and friend who was looking for a woman like Norma. In early 1970, Norma met with Coffee and fellow attorney Sarah Waddington, who had a plan to legally challenge and overturn Texas' restrictive abortion law in federal court but needed a plaintiff who wanted a legal abortion and could not afford to get one.

Norma wanted her identity to remain hidden to protect her daughter, Melissa McCorvey. Coffee assigned Norma the pseudonym of "Jane Roe" and filed the Class Action lawsuit in federal district court on March 3, 1973

Coffee named Dallas district attorney Henry Wade as the defendant. By then, Norma was six months pregnant. She continued to live anonymously in Dallas and was not involved with the court proceedings. According to Joshua Prager, a journalist with access to McCorvey's records, she had given birth, and the baby was adopted by the time the court delivered its verdict on June 17, 1970.

The court struck down Texas's abortion law but did not issue an injunction to prevent the State from enforcing the law they just declared unconstitutional. This combination allowed Coffee and Weddington to appeal the decision directly to the United States Supreme Court.

The U.S. Supreme Court announced its historic ruling on January 22, 1973. McCorvey went public as "Jane Roe" four days later. By then, she was in a long-term relationship with her domestic partner, Connie Gonzales, with whom she lived and had a cleaning and painting business.

However, Norma remained out of the public eye until the decision' tenth anniversary in 1983. In 1985, she spoke out against violence targeting abortion clinics after twenty-seven abortion clinics, including six in Texas, were fire-bombed or set on fire in 1984.

Norma retold her story to numerous reporters and women's rights groups but rarely told it the same way twice. In September 1987, he recanted that a rape led to her pregnancy in the Rape case.

In the late 1980's," McCorvey became an activist, which provided her with income and attention as well as threats and intimidation. In 1989, four days after someone allegedly shot at her and Gonzalez in their Dallas home, she spoke at a prominent abortion rights rally in Washington, D. C., and met Gloria Allred.

Allred, a civil rights attorney, became a friend who helped her curtail her drug and alcohol use and navigate the world of media and fundraising. That year, NBC produced a made-for-television biopic that starred actress Holly Hunter, who won an Emmy for her portrayal of McCorvey. Norma received a percentage of the film's gross.

In 1993, she signed a book deal with Harper Collins to publish her life story in I Am Roe. She also used her fame to raise funds for her Jane Roe Foundation to "help poor Texas women obtain legal abortions" and later the Jane Roe Women's Center. Both were short-lived.

Her view on abortion shifted in 1995 after she met Phillip "Flip" Benham. He was an evangelical preacher and the executive director of Operation Rescue, a national anti-abortion organization, which opened an office next door to the Dallas women's clinic where McCorvey volunteered.

In August, Benham baptized her. Covered by ABC News, the event received international attention; in the months following, she renounced same-sex attraction, publicly reversed her position on abortion, and started working for Operation Rescue.

On this very day, 1 million, three hundred and 59 thousand 4 hundred legal prenatalcides were performed somewhere in the U.S. by women who permitted life to be legally snatched out of their womb, denouncing a life never to be revived, reversed, or in other words, saved!

According to her second autobiography, Won by Love 1997, McCorvey and Gonzalez's relationship had been platonic since 1992, but they continued to live together as friends.

Now an anti-abortion activist, McCorvey claimed she had been manipulated by Coffee and Weddington and poorly treated by the pro-choice movement. She protested at abortion clinics in Dallas and spoke at rallies and demonstrations. She also helped establish Roe No More Ministry, which paid her an annual salary of $40,000; yet in 1997, 1 million, 335 thousand, four hundred prenatalcides continued throughout the United States! Benham served as her advisor and helped her negotiate an $80,000 book deal with Thomas Nelson Publishing that resulted in Won by Love.

In 1996 and 1998, as 1 million 3 hundred - 19 thousand prenatalcides were performed all over the United States, she urged the United States Senate and the U. S Supreme Court to reverse the Roe v. Wade decision. She also converted to Roman Catholicism and traveled internationally to speak to Catholic organizations.

In 2009, 1 million 150 thousand 6 hundred legal estimated prenatalcides continued as the year grew to its end; as she was arrested for disrupting the Senate hearings for Sonia Sotomayor's appointment to the U. S. Supreme Court, and during the 2012 presidential election, she appeared in television ads against the re-election of Barack Obama as sadly another year millions of prenatalcides were performed all over the United States.

Norma McCorvey moved to Smithville, Texas, in 2009 and appeared in Doonby in 2013 as the world continued to practice the law of her mouth as the numbers seemed to lower. Yet, nearly a million prenatalcides were going strong by the year's end.

Doonby is a film made in Smithville by actor John Schneider and his San Antonio-based company, Faith Works Productions.

February 18, 2017, all 862,320 documented pulsating chambers of live conceptions were still being destroyed in clinics all around the U.S. These lives within the womb died within the 24 hours of the very Saturday after Norma's lengthy illness, Norma Leah Nelson's own heart stopped beating at the age of 69 in Katy, Texas!

Norma McCorvey died of a heart that failed to love and be loved; all the 64 million babies in the world died from not being loved by her, being 1 in 75.6 million conceptions. After her death, she again made news. In the 2020 documentary AKA Jane Roe, filmed during her final months of life, an ill McCorvey gave what she called her "deathbed confession." She stated that she had always supported abortion rights and that her role with anti-abortion groups was "all an act" for which she was paid as more than 64 million prenatalcides paid their lives for the support of one in 64 million Norma McCorvey's payment.

A Time For Every Purpose Under The Sun

There is nothing new under the sun; what is to come has been before in another time in history, and history repeats itself and reverses itself all in time. There is a time of peace, then sudden destruction. There is a place where a beating heart is detected.

There is no safer haven than that within the crested womb of time, under the beating heart of the pregnant woman, cradling the pulsating new conception synchronized life under her own heart. Until out of Norma's own misery, reflecting doom upon other lives of so many miserable women who conceived and damned the detecting of a beating heart to silence, never be heard again in their womb or in this world to be born!

Killing the unborn is a common health intervention. Killing an unborn prenatal life is safe when conducted using a method recommended by WHO and by someone with the necessary skills. 6 out of 10 of all unintended pregnancies end in an induced prenatal killing.

By January 22, 1973, the US population was 211.9 million; baby boomers were booming their springs when the US Supreme Court issued a decision in favor of a fundamental right to choose whether to have abortions without excessive government restriction and striking down Texas's abortion ban as unconstitutional.

Let me remind you: abortion is a War on humanity. Certain acts are purposefully committed by a state or on behalf of a state as part of a widespread or systematic policy, typically directed against civilians in times of war or peace.

The violent nature of such acts is considered a severe breach of human rights, hence the name. They differ from war crimes because they are not isolated as committed by individual soldiers but are acts committed in furtherance of a state or organizational policy.

The first prosecution for crimes against humanity took place at the Nuremberg trials. Initially being considered for legal use, widely in international law, following the Holocaust, a global standard of human rights was articulated in the Universal Declaration of Human Rights in 1948.

Political groups or states that violate or incite violation of human rights norms, as found in the Declaration, express the political pathologies associated with crimes against humanity.

War against humanity refers to specific crimes committed in the context of a large-scale attack targeting civilians, regardless of their nationality. These wars include murder, torture, sexual violence, enslavement, persecution, enforced disappearance, etc. Birth control is a war against the conception of humanity; Abortion is a war against the birth of humanity.

The land of the free, home of the brave, was also the land of war on humanity within the womb; over 64 billion babies within their mothers' wombs were thrust into, pickled, and brimmed with salt, crushed, and often cast away into dumpsters or sold to cosmetic companies from 1973-2021!

Women were given the law within their own hands as judges who gave the death penalty to every innocent baby. The Bible-toting Christian would not have loved the sweet Baby Jesus. A 10 -12-year-old virgin Mary would be sent to a clinic such as in Indiana to go through an abortion if she were pregnant within the last days in the 49 years of "Pro-Choice!"

The men in the Churches of today would want to crucify him, and the women would cry "abort" him. The church is full of birth control, such as tubal, vasectomies, IUDs, patches, pills, and condoms that prevent their child from being conceived, an assortment of evils from A to Z!

Who knows what brilliant minds have been destroyed by the selfish, demanding, and greediness of evil, murderous premeditation of would-be parents? Jesus nearly got Mary put to death by the man she was espoused to, but at the end of the day, she was not stoned. Today, Jesus is aborted over 63 million times in the wombs of every pro-choice woman running wild and rapid across the U.S. with the blood of the cross on her hands, suffering and forbidding the little children.

Why were these homicides made legal? Every abortion seemed right in the eyes of each woman: kill, steal the fruit of the womb, and destroy it. Now understand how a woman will devour and eat the flesh of her child; it is served as the feast of abortion.

We won't mention the vanity creams produced with the placenta of the afterbirth. Adolf Hitler killed openly, but women disquietly went into a clinic and committed her iniquity behind the closed doors of the law. Oh, the suffering little children!

They shall be justified in time! Since 2000, the middle class has shrunk, yet there is more debt, working longer, living longer, and entering retirement. Some 85% of those who describe themselves as middle class say it is more difficult now than it was ten years ago to maintain their standard of living.

The boomer effect refers to the influence of the generation born between 1946 and 1964 on the economy and most markets. The term is used to describe everything related to baby boomers, including their consumer habits, social media preferences, how marketers target the boomer generation, and how the financial services sector can best serve boomers as their priorities shift in later life.

The boomer effect is sometimes called the boomer factor or the boomer shift. Baby boomers hold a large amount of the wealth in the U.S., making them a prime market segment. Baby boomers, stand tall! This is our moment. The silent generation members, Gen Xers!

How convenient and how slick for the abortion law to help the millions of unwed mothers stay in their new jobs! The oldest baby boomers born in 1946 are old enough to work; a Gen Xer or two on the payroll will be heading to file their taxes. The supreme act of selflessness: boomers pay more in income taxes than any other generation.

This is where the government is having a cocktail party, taking out taxes on all of those baby boomers working in those fast-food chain restaurants up and down busy four-corner streets. The government may have gotten a bit like a spoiled child in a candy store.

The government does not have to imagine fanaticizing over 78 million baby boomers eventually working on a job and being taxed. By 1964, the first crop of taxed income had begun to grow. Every year, the crop increased; fields grew as acres and acres of bountiful, beautiful human beings, earning minimal wages of dollars but making billions for the government.

In 1964, the government was viewing 10,000 baby boomers turning 18 every day, the sheer size of that generation putting money into the government.

The economy grew interested in every check of every baby boomer in the U.S. from 1965- when the first baby boomer became hired until the last of them retires in 2030, or maybe until they become too ill to work or die.

The government became like a spoiled child for 30 years, taking money out of the wages of millions of baby boomer's paychecks until the first retirement began. Each day, since 2006, the oldest baby boomers began to retire.

This generation that changed the world in many ways is now about to leave its stamp on retirement, boosting demand for investment opportunities in health care, elder care, medical devices, and related industries that cater to that demographic.

Quick, there was a reason the retirement age was changed for women; in 1961, the same extension was applied for men to retire at 62. set back to 62, then 65, again, the retirement age was 67, and now there is a chance of never retiring until sickness or death!

The government now needed the ever-increasing retiring baby boomers to stay in their jobs...Why? Uncle Sam needs more than a few good men; Uncle Sam needs women too; Uncle Sam needs "YOU" working, owing, and paying those taxes!

A Time To Speak, Mend

On Friday, June 24, 2022, the Supreme Court said it had voted to overturn Roe vs. Wade, the ruling that in 1973 declared abortion a constitutional right. The court has thereby torn up a right it granted almost half a century ago, stripping away women's blood bath of premeditated judgments to be right, creating a seismic political and societal shift throughout the United States.

15 States passed new laws regulating access to abortion in 2022. States mimicking Texas' 2021 fetal heartbeat Law. Idaho and Oklahoma passed laws based on Texas' 2021 fetal heartbeat law, which prohibits abortion if a fetal heartbeat is detected. According to the US National Library of Medicine's public encyclopedia, "most often, the heartbeat cannot be heard or seen on an ultrasound until at least 6 to 7 weeks."

Texas law allows private citizens to sue abortion providers or anyone else who assists a person receiving an abortion, such as drivers to a clinic or anyone who financially assists the abortion.

Oklahoma's Heartbeat Act, or SB 1503, bans abortions after a heartbeat is detected in the fetus. Like the Texas law, it allows private citizens to file civil lawsuits against those who provide or assist in an abortion.

In comparison, Idaho's SB 1309 allows only family members of the aborted fetus to sue the abortion provider for damages of $20,000 or more. Idaho and Texas provide exemptions for medical emergencies and pregnancies related to rape or incest.

Restrictions on methods of abortion or access to abortions: Florida passed a 15-week ban on abortion in April. The bill allows pregnant people to get an abortion only for cases that pose a "serious risk" to the pregnant person's health or involve a fetal anomaly. The law also requires the abortion and the reason it was performed to be reported to the state. The bill does not include an exemption for rape or incest.

Arizona also passed a 15-week abortion ban this year. The law makes exceptions for life-threatening pregnancies and those that may result in "substantial and irreversible impairment" of a pregnant person's "major bodily functions." There is no exception for cases of rape or incest. Kentucky's House Bill 3 outlaws abortion after 15 weeks of pregnancy. It also requires patients who receive abortions to file "birth-death certificates." Doctors who perform abortions must report each procedure to the state, along with the method of abortion and detailed information about the pregnant person and their sexual partner.

Depending on which provisions of the law are violated,

abortion providers can risk civil penalties, felony charges, or the loss of their medical license. The law makes an exception for medical emergencies. There is no exception for cases of rape or incest.

Indiana passed a law requiring medical personnel to ask pregnant persons seeking an abortion whether they were coerced into that decision.

In 2021, eight states passed restrictions on access to abortion through medication, including South Dakota. A 2022 South Dakota law further restricted access to abortion through medication. It requires pregnant persons seeking an abortion through medication to get a minimum of three appointments before getting all the needed drugs.

Restrictions on abortion based on fetal genetic abnormalities: West Virginia passed the Unborn Child with Down Syndrome Protection and Education Act, prohibiting abortions because of physical and intellectual disabilities. Physicians must confirm the patient is not seeking an abortion for these reasons.

"Trigger" laws banning abortion: Some states have laws on the books that ban abortion in the state if the Supreme Court overturns Roe v. Wade. These statutes are also called "trigger" laws.

Wyoming passed a law that would outlaw abortion five days after the Supreme Court overturned Roe v. Wade. The bill makes exceptions for pregnancies resulting from rape or incest and for cases when an abortion is necessary to preserve the pregnant person from "a serious risk of death or of substantial and irreversible physical impairment of a major bodily function."

There are currently 12 other states with abortion ban "trigger" laws in place.

Total abortion bans:

Oklahoma also passed SB 612 criminally banning abortion procedures within the state. Doctors can only perform abortions in medical emergencies. The law makes performing an abortion or attempting to perform one a felony punishable by a maximum fine of $100,000, a maximum of 10 years in state prison, or both. The law does not provide exceptions in cases of rape or incest.

States expanding abortion access:

Six states have passed new abortion laws in 2022 that protect access to the procedure.

Colorado, New Jersey, and Washington all passed laws that either establish or expand statutory protections for abortion access. The Reproductive Health Equity Act. in Colorado affirms that pregnant people have the right to an abortion in the state and blocks public entities from denying or restricting that right.

The Freedom of Reproductive Choice Act in New Jersey codifies the right to an abortion in the state. It also permits the State Department of Banking and Insurance to conduct a study on whether the cost of an abortion is a barrier to low-income and uninsured women.

Washington state passed a bill in March preventing the state from penalizing, prosecuting, or taking action against anyone who pets an abortion or who assists someone who does. The law is a direct response to states such as Texas that allow civil suits against abortion providers or those who assist a pregnant person in getting an abortion.

Maryland and Washington passed laws expanding the

number of medical professionals who can perform abortions in both states.

In California, Maryland, and Oregon, the legislation requires health care plans to cover abortion or establishes a state fund to assist with abortion costs.

Connecticut's House Bill 5414:

Protects abortion providers and those who help someone get an abortion in Connecticut from being sued in another state.

When will the Supreme Court decide the constitutionality of abortion?

The Supreme Court's final ruling on the Mississippi case- which will determine if abortion is a federally protected right – is expected to come out before the end of the term, in late June or early July.

A Season And A Time To Be Born!

As our nation prepares to ring in the new year, the U.S. Census Bureau projects the United States population will be 332,403,650 on January 1, 2022. This represents a 0.21% increase in population or an additional 706,899 people since New Year's Day 2021. December 30, 2021.

The current population in the United States is 335,024,310 as of Thursday morning, July 21, 2022. 2, 620,650 babies were born within the first 6 months of this year! Nearly 3.7 million babies were born in the US in 2021; that's about 46,000 more than were born in 2020, but the 1% increase still put the number short of 2019 levels.

US birth rates went up for 1st time since 2014. The number of babies born in the U.S. rose 1% last year after seeing a 2% decrease in 2020, according to a new federal report. Before this report, the number of births had been decreasing by an average of 2% per year.

The report did not explain why the number of births increased, but Pew Research Center polls have suggested Americans delayed having babies during the first year of the pandemic due to public health and economic uncertainty, so the rising number could be the result of a rebound.

"When it comes to changes in fertility behavior, we're limited," Dr. Brady Hamilton, from the NCHS Division of Vital Statistics and lead author of the report, told ABC News. "That's where you need a survey about what's behind the decision-making process."

The report also showed the fertility rate—the number of live births per 1,000 women between the ages 15 and 44—was 56.6. This is up from 56 in 2020 and the first increase since 2014, according to the CDC.

However, the total fertility rate—the number of births a

hypothetical group of 1,000 people would have over their lifetimes—was 1,663.5 births per 1,000 women.

This is still below what experts refer to as replacement level, the level a population needs to replace itself, which is 2,100 births per 1,000 women.

The team looked at how birth rates among women aged 25 and older increased while decreasing for those aged 24 and younger. "That sort of suggests when we saw the decline in births from 2019 to 2020, probably a lot of births were postponed," Hamilton said. "People were waiting to see what happened with the pandemic, and rates rose among older women as they may have proceeded to have that child."

Among teenagers aged 15 to 19, the rate of birth declined 6% from 15.4 per 1,000 to 14.4 per 1,000—a record low for this age group. Teenage births have been continuously falling since 2007 by an average of 7% through last year. "When you look at it across time, that's a 77% decline since 1991 and a 65% decline since 2017. "That's astonishing," Hamilton said. "That's certainly good news, and it will be interesting to see when we go into next year if it continues."

Meanwhile, for tweens and teens aged 10 to 14, the rate of birth was 0.2 per 1,000, which is unchanged since 2015, the report found. Additionally, researchers also looked at births by race and found that white and Hispanic women each saw the number of births increase by about 2% from 2020 to 2021.

Meanwhile, Black and Asian women saw the number of births decline by 2.4% and 2.5%, respectively, over the same period, while American Indian/Alaskan Native women saw their numbers fall by 3.2%.

This report also examined the type of delivery and how early the babies were born. Data showed that 32.1% of babies were born via cesarean delivery in 2021, up from 31.8% in 2020 and the second increase in a row after the rates had declined from 2009 to 2019.

The percentage of C-sections increased among all racial and ethnic groups, with the highest seen among Black women, from 36.3% to 36.8%. While C-sections can lower the risk of death in women with high-risk pregnancies, they are associated with complications such as infection or blood clots, according to the Cleveland Clinic.

The preterm birth rate also rose by 4% in 2021, from 10.09% to 10.48%, which is the highest reported rate since 2007. Increases were seen in babies born early preterm, which is before 34 weeks gestation, and later preterm, which is 34 to 37 weeks gestation.

Premature babies are at a greater risk for problems with feeding, breathing, vision, and hearing, as well as behavioral issues. Whenever you see an increase in preterm births, that's concerning; an increase in healthy-term babies are at greater risk than later-term babies of not surviving the first year of life.

It may not be clear what's behind the rise in preterm birth rates, but it is said that mothers younger than 18 and older than 35 are more likely to have premature babies. There was an increase in older moms' birth rates.

Abortion rates in the United States have been falling steadily for decades, long before restrictive statutes began to make the procedure difficult to obtain in some areas. Experts say access to better birth control is one of the main reasons.

Abortions in the U.S. peaked in 1981 at a rate of 29.3%

per 1,000 women between the ages of 15 and 44, according to the Centers for Disease Control and Prevention. Since then, the number has fallen by three-fifths.

In 2019, the last year for which numbers are available, the rate was 11.4 %. The decline has been seen in almost all states, regardless of whether abortion access was restricted, but that could change if the sweeping protections of Roe Vs. Wade are overturned!

Research has shown that increases in distance to clinics are associated with lower abortion rates, especially for women with limited resources and difficult personal circumstances. The vast majority of women in states where abortion likely would be banned or strictly limited would have to travel several hundred miles or more to reach a provider.

It has been estimated about two-thirds of women in those states would find a way to reach an open facility, but one-third would not, resulting in an estimated 75,000 fewer abortions per year. In 2019, at least 629,898 abortions were reported in the United States, according to the CDC.

A DECADES-LONG-FIGHT TO UPEND ROE VS. WADE

In the United States, each year, about half of pregnancies are unintended, and about 40% of these lead to abortion. America is in the midst of a birth rate crisis, having now reached its lowest level in nearly half a century.

Many factors are contributing to this trend: people choosing to have children later in life, declining sperm counts as a result of environmental toxins, the growing wealth gap, recent shifts in how we work due to the pandemic, and stress.

Whatever the reasons, declining birth rates are a reality we must accept. If the trend continues, it will only take a few decades before a small number of young people are economically supporting a vastly larger aging population.

This will bring ruin to our nation's programs and will either force immense technological innovation or the bankruptcy of our country. While the government has little control over the cultural factors affecting declining U.S. birth rates, there is one key thing the government can do to perhaps system the tide: force insurers to cover fertility care-much like the Mental Health Parity and Addiction Equity Act mandated coverage for mental illnesses.

Working from states and the federal government to bring real change; Our economic future is at stake if we don't start making more babies! The states on their level come together as the majority ruling on new mandates.

Having children intrinsically is part of what defines our purpose in life. Fortunately, states are starting to realize these things, and some are taking action. This is an issue of national importance and given the "avalanche effect" of declining birth rates, our government needs to reverse this trend now if we are to remain a vibrant nation. The time has come for Congress and the president to construct and sign into law a fertility care mandate for all health insurance plans in the United States. Such a mandate would broaden access and break the monopoly presently killing off the future of The United States in the womb!

Baby boomers hold a large amount of the wealth in the U.S., making them a prime market segment. Baby boomers are gradually retiring, boosting demand for and investment opportunities in healthcare, elder care, medical devices, and related industries that cater to that demographic.

There has been expressed concern about the trickle-down economic effects as boomers reach their later years. The impact on the economy and the labor force baby boomers are expected to have as they reach retirement age.

The U.S. needs high growth and economic boom; this is prosperity for the nation, which can only happen at the birth of our children.

As more than 250,000 Americans are estimated to celebrate their 65th birthdays each month, heading toward retirement, the impact on the labor force and consumer spending is already showing profound effects.

The cause of lower labor numbers can be chalked up to boomers who, though many were forced to work extra years to compensate for retirement investments lost in the 2008-2009 market crash, are now retiring in significant numbers.

As boomers retire, expect wide-ranging effects: Not only do retirees produce and contribute less in an economic sense, but they also tend to spend less, which is a recipe for economic growth. One area where this generation is spending more is on their adult children. A substantial percentage of parents are providing some financial support for their adult children, with student loan assistance being a significant area of financial burden.

For many boomers, that financial assistance goes beyond helping out with student loans to assist in providing housing. In February 2020, 47% of young adults aged 18 to 29 resided with one or both of their parents. As of July 2020, that number had surged to 52%- surpassing the previous peak last seen during the GREAT DEPRESSION!

Between bleak economic predictions, widespread post-recession losses of retirement savings, and the subprime mortgage debacle, it is no wonder some members of this generation are reluctant to retire. Even now, the generation that coined the phrase "live to work" is living up to its reputation.

This workplace longevity may prove a problem for younger workers who have struggled to find well-paid, stable work during their lives of high unemployment. The upside? Retirement for this cohort is as inevitable as the boomerang effect that will eventually create job availability.

Ultimately, some boomers take the live-to-work ethos to an extreme. A 2013 Gallup poll, which investigated the consumer and workplace behaviors of baby boomers, posed the following question: "State what age you plan to retire?" For 10% of respondents, the answer was a succinct "Never!"

The bottom line is while baby boomers are working longer, their inevitable retirement will have widespread effects on the American economy already being seen now. There are high impacts on consumer spending, as retirees not only produce less but also consume and spend less. While the workforce participation rate already sits at historically low levels, the mass retirements of boomers are having a negative boomerang effect- essentially leaving jobs empty as younger employees are not qualified for these jobs or not willing to work on these jobs.

A law and a mandate have the same power to be enforced, The only difference is how it came to be. A law is passed by the Senate and the House of Representatives and signed by the governor. A mandate is made by the governor, with the power given to them by the legislature in a state of emergency.

AMERICA'S BIRTH RATE IS NOW A NATIONAL EMERGENCY!

The new birth rate numbers are out, and they're a disaster. There are now only 59.6 births per 1,000 women, the lowest rate ever recorded in the United States. Some of the decrease is due to good news. This is the continuing decline of teen pregnancies, but most of it is due to people getting married later and choosing to have fewer children, and the worst part is everyone is treating this news with a shrug. Birth control and abortion are the main problems.

It wasn't always his way. It used to be taken for granted that the best indicator of a nation's health was its citizens' desire and capacity to reproduce. And it should still seem self-evident that people's willingness to have children is not only a sign of confidence in the future but a sign of cultural health. It's a signal that people are willing to commit to the most enduring responsibility on Earth, which is raising their children.

National health is displayed in reproduction, both in the reproduction of babies and in dollars and cents! The nation of today is in a reproduction disaster; the sense of it all is the birth of pride. Pride is before destruction and a haughty spirit before a fall. The vanity of pride is beautiful in one own eye; refusing to accept that beauty fades gives a haughtiness that causes a blindsided fall. The blind can't lead the blind; they both fall into the ditch.

Today, we see the problems wrought by the decline in productive population all over the industrialized world, where polities are ripping each other to shreds over how to pay for various forms of entitlements, especially for old people.

The debates play out in diverse ways in different countries, but in other ways, they are exactly the same. That's because they are ruled by the same ruthlessness: the fewer young, productive people you have to pay for entitlements for old, unproductive people, the steeper the bill for the entire society becomes. This basic problem is strangling Europe's economies. While the United States is among the least bad of the bunch, it is still headed in the wrong direction.

It doesn't have to be this way. While the evidence for government programs that encourage people to have more children is mixed, the fact of the matter is that 40% of women have fewer children than they want to.

Like a thief and a robber in the night, our future has nearly been stolen from Americans right under our own eyes with our own selfish, demanding ways. America is known as the melting pot of the world, but somehow, a leak has sprung in the bucket; the pot's water has been nearly vaporized. The water is nearly gone; the U.S. is thirsty; the thirst for life, new life, is about to kill us.

When did the hole begin? Years ago! Common sense here would help to solve the problems of today that began 20 years ago! It's not so hard to understand; without babies being born, there is no future. If females continue the way they are now, by 2030, there will be no future with children of just eight or so years old. Children are our future! Children lead the way; children grow up to be leaders and presidents of the U.S. By the year 2040, how many 18-year-olds will there be? Don't count on a new crop of "BABY BOOMERS" from this generation; it's too late for a mature, professional harvest to be expected until 2060!

One baby out of 76.4 million persuaded the U.S. to pass a law legalizing women to premeditate and commit more than 69 estimated million prenatalcide deaths! This one baby grew up to be the woman with the negative impact of the destruction of our nation within 18 years after her death. She is dead today, but the wrath of her fire has torched our nation's fields of grain.

Many wombs are empty vessels, which danced to the music and played to be seduced to the pleasure of wine and the good life in "night-clubs" now the same beat and music and dance the same dance in "day-clubs" called Church-centers! Just a place where everyone craves to be seen and heard, like children needing attention!

Where are the children? 40% were slaughtered in the war of ROE VS. WADE. ROE VS. WADE has torched our American fields and trampled our harvest; our fruit has been crushed on the vines in the nation's wombs. ROE VS. WADE turns its ugly cheek, where are the children's laughter? Children, indeed, are our future, but where are the children of our future in the U.S.?

Statistics reveal the population of 166.24 million females in the U.S., 82% of those females are the childbearing ages 15-49 also using birth control: this number also includes the 1.6 million (6% teenagers and 5% adults) that are GLBQT. It figures to understand 166.24 million females minus 82% leaves just a small percentage of females (18%) that are not using any form or type of means of birth control to resist having a booming number of 18-year-olds for the work/employment year of 2040! The statistics did not reveal if these 18% of non-birth control users would have an abortion if they did get pregnant, but the question is, can 18% of the United States produce 75.6 million babies in 18 years?

The U.S. needs a replay of 1946-1964 today to baby boom America again! But in 1973, a sabotaging war began. What is sabotage? Sabotage means to deliberately destroy, damage, or obstruct (something), especially for political, military, social, or personal advantage. Norma Leah McCorvey never was known to abort any of her own 3 pregnancies, even though she wanted to.

Norma may not have known anything about sabotage, but while she carried her children to term and gave them up for adoption, her team of lawyers took our nation's 64 million babies to court, found, and charged them guilty of being conceived, guilty for being unwanted by their mothers.

The capital punishment was for them all to be sucked apart- or torn limb by limb, beheaded, salted, butchered, debrained, stabbed until the doctors noted they were dead; 64 million perished without knowledge; our great nation was sabotaged for 50 years until 2022 when Roe v. Wade was overturned!

Sabotage began with ROE VS. WADE; that is how to sabotage a nation. At first, it may look like a big party, just a big celebration; it took years before the party began to look like a parting, and the celebration more like cells (babies)-brat (a medical term for banana, rice, applesauce, and toast given for an upset stomach)! It does take a medical doctor to understand; there is no pun intended here.

Bration- the medical term for the removal or destruction of a body part, tissue, or function (Celebration) cells or the removal or destruction of a baby. ROE VS. WADE was all about medically "Celebrating" the hearts of 1.6 billion babies of our nation while the whole world simply partied and celebrated!

Because of your mutation and befouling of your bodies and the fruit of your seed, the stench has become a reproach unto the Divine will! "People are destroyed for lack of knowledge; the Divine will also reject the disobedient and the proud; that thou shalt be no priest to me: seeing thou hast forgotten, I will also forget thy children." Hosea 4:6

The U.S. is and has been at war, under an attack at the very core of the people by their own hands—a praying nation on its knees, begging for mercy and justice. The rights of Christian Women are being taken away; it's a shame. The consonances of church members are all sad; shoulders appear heavily laden and with a bowed down head. ROE VS. WADE has been overturned; the church members murmuring in prayers for their God to move into the courthouse.

Are you serious? Sister woman, where is your spirit of virtue? Did I understand you right? You going to pray for what? And over who's rights? Women's or babies? Let's remember our ways are not like the DIVINEWILL, neither are our thoughts pure; the DIVINEWILL is not a mind to think or wonder, the DIVINEWILL does not change. The DIVINE Will IS Spirit THAT WILLS Change! The Divine will is an involuntary action!

The DIVINEWILL is not submissive to the desires of our heart, knowledge of our mind, or our physical strength.

Many Soulless, heartless people without compassion are stunned by this impartial "DIVINEWILL." The DIVINEWILL wills even the percentage of a man's penis and reproduction system as well as a female's vagina and female's reproduction system; the body belongs to the DIVINEWILL, not just these small parts belong to DIVINEWILL; the DIVINEWILL requires a tenth of our bodies as tithes; our genitals are truly private parts! Our whole body belongs to the DIVINEWILL!

It is our reasonable portion of service. (holding nothing back.) The man's sperms are the seeds of righteousness, the planting of the DIVINEWILL, and the female's ovum is the Soul house of the DIVINEWILL of life.

How have the people robbed The DIVINEWILL? By not presenting their bodies as living testaments and whole unto Him. The womb is where the life of every living person began, but let's take a religious view into the congregation that is meant to be kept secret. Churches open every Sunday with pews filled with people worshiping in lip praise, show, and tithes (worldly offerings). Yet the scripture reads ye have robbed the Spirit in tithes and offering. No, not of money, not of food, but of the obedience to give what belongs to the Spirit. We all are 1 Spirit conceived within our mother's wombs; our bodies' involuntary actions belong to the Divine Will. Conception is the life Will of a Spirit in transit to this plane. Every female is gifted with the legacy of eggs passed down from generation into her womb at conception; there is a plan for those eggs! The predestination of conception is placed by the Divine will; conception is either a blessing or a trapping!

When a female looks at a conception as a trapping, to

her, it is not a blessing; she is caught in an act that was only meant for pleasure. The Divinewill is not mocked; the unity between a man and woman is undefiled, meaning you can't curse what is blessed, and what is a blessing can't be cursed.

The only thing that Wills intimacy between a male and a woman blessed is if the Divine will join their spirits' together before they even touch. Without their spirits being joined, they are never blessed to be together, and this is the beginning of an unhappy relationship, whether it be a lawful marriage or not. The law can't give faith, neither can marriage make one faithful: only the joining of the spirit is the beginning of love, and this is a gift from the Divine will.

A Time That Men Should Fear (Respect) Before The Divine Will!

Dearly beloved and bereaved, we have gathered here today to discuss the news on the world broadcast system this month of July 2022. This is a sermon for Sunday morning at your church. Isaiah 64:6 says, "Come just as you are, as a wretch; as an unclean thing, knowing all our righteousness's are as filthy rags, and all do fade as a leaf; and our iniquities, like the wind, have taken us away."

You're in the right place for sin-sick, disobedient people; churches are hospitals where everyone is contagious with something that can and will attack the person next to you, just like COVID-19, but covering yourself with a mask will not protect you. Give me a microphone, and never mind the pulpit; too many have already "pulled blood deep into the pit!" I'm not expecting an offering so I can speak the truth and walk out before the doors of the church open and certainly before you start chanting and walking me out.

No man can save himself, not even your Pastor, and as much as we love our children, we can't save them from themselves. I know the Bible says to save yourselves from this untoward generation of vipers, but the vipers are where the judgment starts in the church and begins with the Pastor. Actually, spiritual judgment starts in the home with every child and their parents. Disobedience sown in the dishonoring of children towards parents leading to fear, doubt and unbelief, sickness, disease, and the ultimate sacrifice of death!

I'm not going to keep you long, but you can keep your reaction prayers until after the communion has been omitted because many are sick among you from taking too much of this blood communion already unworthily! Just get some water; and no, it's not holy water, just H2O from the lakes and rivers that have drained from the sewers and the sinks of homes and clinics, etc., and manufactured into those water bottles that are nothing more than tap water!

A Christian research group has released the findings of a national survey containing a startling revelation: 70% of women who have abortions in the U.S. are Christians, and 23% of those women identify as Evangelical Christians.

The survey, which polled 1,038 women who'd had abortions from across the U.S., found that almost 40% of those women were attending a Christian church once a month or more at the time of their abortion. However, a majority of the women who attended church regularly kept their abortions a secret from their church community, mostly out of fear of being judged or condemned. Fear is not a gift from the Spirit.

Throwing rocks and hiding their hands? A journalist and activist witnessed an anti-abortion picketer come into a clinic, have an abortion, and go back to picketing again.

There was really no place to hide from the eye of the Spirit. Christian anti-choices do far more harm than good, as the wine presses are wet and trampled with the blood of the children on their hands.

Remember Revelation 14:20. The blind can't lead the blind; the proud and the haughty, the pastors and their disciples. Have you read Psalms 118:8, Micah 7:5, Jeremiah 17:5, and Galatians 6:3?

1 Peter 4:17 states that Pastors and their whole congregation are under judgment; Judgment begins in the House of the Lord, beginning with every Pastor! There is a time and a season for every purpose under heaven; it has come for the time to heal from ROE VS. WADE, but first, this nation must repent!

2 Chronicles 7:14 says, "If my people, which are called by my name, shall humble themselves, and pray, and seek my face, and turn from their wicked ways; then will I hear from heaven, and will forgive their sin, and will heal their land."

The loss of our aborted children has been buried under a weighted cloak of sin; they perished without honor. Who shall plead for the aborted children? Deuteronomy 28 shall happen if thou shalt hearken diligently; a cursing or a blessing has been set before the nation whether it shall hear or forbear.

Nahum 3:1 says, "Woe to the bloody city!"

Ezekiel 22:1-4 states, "Moreover the word of the Lord came unto me, saying, Now, thou son of man, wilt thou judge the bloody city? Yes, thou shalt show her all her abominations. Then say thou, Thus saith the Lord God, the city sheddeth blood in the midst of it. Thou art become guilty in thy blood that thou hast shed, and hast defiled thyself in thine idols which thou hast made, and thou hast caused thy days to draw near, and art come even unto thy years; therefore have I made thee a reproach unto the heathen, and a mocking to all countries."

What's done is done but not forgotten; overturning ROE VS. WADE will not allow the nation to grow a new crop in our fields before 2030! The clock of time is ticking; the time to baby boom America back again is now under judgment!

But the judgment of God has long been overlooked; the wrath has long been hot! Exodus 22:22-24 speaks of the judgment revenging eye for an eye. What is raiment? Cloth or robe; we each have a beautiful protective garment for our spirit! The Spirit has given us all a raiment of skin: this raiment is the very conception that we all begin with, which for countless millions has been aborted. The very covering of their spirit was taken, and for years, they have cried for their recompense! How long will the blood of the innocent be thought to be silent?

The nation's population of 332,403,650 U.S. citizens, 83.4% confessing Christians that pray religiously in sanctuaries are indeed among the 166 million Christian women who practice birth control.

John 10:10 says, "The thief cometh not, but for to steal, and to kill, and to destroy; I am come that they might have life and that they might have it more abundantly." Let's define "Destroy" as the action or process of causing so much damage to something that it no longer exists or cannot be repaired. Let's define another word, "Destruction" - Put an end to the existence of (something) by damaging or attacking it.

Because destruction is the work of Satan, death is the end result of his sinister plans. Just as he deceived Adam in the garden, his destroying vanity of greed for selfish power is still spreading like wildfire in the world as we know it today. Cain slew Adam and Eve's son Abel, but there was life in the womb, and the seed of Adam was alive and well.

But unlike today, the Church has all but gone to the pit! The fire has been lit for the sacrifices to the sex Gods of the ancient Molech (Leviticus 20:20) and is unknowingly practiced today!

Just take a look at the blood on the altar from the clipped tubes and the fragmented abortions! Tubal ligations, vasectomies, and abortions are all practiced by the Brothers and Sisters sitting in the congregation of the Churches of this nation today!

1 out of 4 females in the congregation of the nation, totaling 11 million women, have their fallopian tubes tied, cut, and burnt. The tubes of 70% of the great congregation have been gutted and left upon the altar as a sacrifice for pleasure. "Tubal" and "ligation" means to tie off. Christians have cut themselves off from the tree of life!

Fallopian tubes are thin tubes that connect each of your ovaries to your uterus—they're passageways for unfertilized eggs. In a tubal ligation, you'll have surgery to cut or block your fallopian tubes. This is mutilation and defiling of the body, rendering it unfit.

Side effects of birth control pills include blood clots, gallbladder disease, heart attack, high blood pressure, mood changes, lack of libido, producing offensive vaginal odor, smelly discharge, dry and thinned out vagina, decreased entrance of the vagina and smaller clitoris; vision problems that include increased risk for glaucoma.

Abortion kills more people than guns; 18 youths daily are killed by guns, 45,222 yearly, but abortion kills 3,500 people daily! There are a variety of diverse ways to end a child's life in the womb of time without morals or conscience. It's hard to believe, but it's true that 70% of these killings are done by the Sister, Mother, and Evangelist and the choir members in the robes in the front of the church and standing at the door is the usher that passes out the fans and the Deaconess that serves the holy communion. Abortion is wrong; it is not a solution to a problem; abortion is an immoral, insensitive, brutal act of murder! The church is full of lost spirits that have been slaughtered by the congregation. Death, hell, and destruction are the sins of the so-called sanctified Holy Ghost, filled with the blood of the 1.5 billion children that were sacrificed at the altar of Molech!

Of course, Pastors preach of the Lamb of God being slain; or did someone misunderstand him to say the lamb of Gog? Or even the child of Molech? None of the procedures below was done at the altar in a Church, but the Christians protocol in the suffering of them all. When you've done it to the least, you did it to them all; when you broke one commandment, you broke them all: thou shall not kill. Which one of the following medical abortions was your choice below?

EARLY NON-SURGICAL (MEDICAL) ABORTION

A drug is given to stop the development of the child. The use of this drug may cause cramping, pelvic pain, or bleeding. Often, women will pass clots, tissue (the nesting of the womb), and then the unborn child within hours or days. This procedure is not without possible effects and immediate medical abortion risks, such as:

- Pelvic infection (sepsis)
- Incomplete abortion
- Blood clots in the uterus
- Heavy bleeding (hemorrhage)
- Cut or torn cervix
- Perforation of the uterus wall
- Anesthesia-related complications
- Rh immune Globulin Therapy (could endanger future pregnancies)

Long-Term Medical Abortion Risks:

- Future childbearing – in some cases, complications associated with abortion may make it difficult or impossible to become pregnant in the future.

Psychological Abortion Risks:

It is important to note that some women encounter a variety of psychological effects after an abortion. These range from irritability, difficulty sleeping, and depression to post-traumatic stress disorder.

Vacuum Aspiration

Performed in weeks 2 to 12 of pregnancy. Requires a local anesthetic injected into or near the cervix. The cervix is then stretched open, allowing a tube to be inserted. The unborn child and placenta are then suctioned out. Occasionally, this is followed by a procedure to scrape the walls of the uterus, making sure it has been completely emptied of the unborn child and placenta. This procedure, considered by some as capital punishment upon the unborn child guilty of not being wanted, comes with risks to the mother. Possible effects and immediate medical abortion risks include:

- Pelvic infection (sepsis)
- Incomplete abortion
- Blood clots in the uterus
- Heavy bleeding (hemorrhage)
- Cut or torn cervix
- Perforation of the uterus wall
- Anesthesia-related complications
- Rh immune Globulin Therapy (could endanger future pregnancies)

Long-Term Medical Abortion Risks:

- Future childbearing – in some cases, complications associated with abortion may make it difficult or impossible to become pregnant in the future.

Psychological Abortion Risks:

It is important to note that some women encounter a variety of psychological effects after an abortion. These range from irritability, difficulty sleeping, and depression to post-traumatic stress disorder.

Dilation And Evacuation (D & C)

Performed in weeks 13 to 21-22 of pregnancy. Sponge-like pieces of material are placed into the cervix, slowly opening the cervix over a period of several hours or overnight. The mother may be given intravenous medications to help with pain and prevent infection. General anesthesia is then given to the mother, and the unborn child and placenta are removed with forceps and suction curettage. Occasionally, it is necessary to dismember the unborn child. This procedure is not without possible effects and immediate medical abortion risks, such as:

- Pelvic infection (sepsis)
- Incomplete abortion
- Blood clots in the uterus
- Heavy bleeding (hemorrhage)
- Cut or torn cervix
- Perforation of the uterus wall
- Anesthesia-related complications
- Rh immune Globulin Therapy (could endanger future pregnancies)

Long-Term Medical Abortion Risks:

- Future childbearing – in some cases, complications associated with abortion may make it difficult or impossible to become pregnant in the future.

Psychological Abortion Risks:

It is important to note that some women encounter a variety of psychological effects after an abortion. These range from irritability, difficulty sleeping, and depression to post-traumatic stress disorder.

Labor Induction

Performed in weeks 13 to 21/22 of pregnancy. This procedure may require a hospital stay. Drugs are given to the mother to terminate the pregnancy and to begin labor (usually starts in 2-4 hours). In the event that the placenta is not completely removed during labor, the cervix must be opened, and a doctor will perform suction curettage. Possible side effects and risks are similar to those of other procedures, including:

- Pelvic infection (sepsis)
- Incomplete abortion
- Blood clots in the uterus
- Heavy bleeding (hemorrhage)
- Cut or torn cervix

- Perforation of the uterus wall
- Anesthesia-related complications
- Rh immune Globulin Therapy (could endanger future pregnancies)

Long-Term Medical Abortion Risks:

- Future childbearing – in some cases, complications associated with abortion may make it difficult or impossible to become pregnant in the future.

Psychological Abortion Risks:

It is important to note that some women encounter a variety of psychological effects after an abortion. These range from irritability, difficulty sleeping, and depression to post-traumatic stress disorder.

Dilation And Extraction (D & X)

Performed in weeks 13 to 21/22 of pregnancy, often referred to as a partial-birth abortion. This type of abortion is illegal except when necessary to save the life of the mother. This is always performed in a hospital and can be done in rare cases after 16 weeks.

The doctor opens the cervix, grasps the unborn child's foot with an instrument (not with a hand), and delivers the child completely, with the exception of the head. An incision is made in the back of the child's head, and a suction tube is inserted. The child's skull is fully suctioned out, allowing the head to collapse. The child is then delivered dead.

The side effects and risks are similar to other procedures, including:

- Pelvic infection (sepsis)
- Incomplete abortion
- Blood clots in the uterus
- Heavy bleeding (hemorrhage)
- Cut or torn cervix
- Perforation of the uterus wall
- Anesthesia-related complications
- Rh immune Globulin Therapy (could endanger future pregnancies)

Long-Term Medical Abortion Risks:

- Future childbearing – in some cases, complications associated with abortion may make it difficult or impossible to become pregnant in the future.

Psychological Abortion Risks:

It is important to note that some women encounter a variety of psychological effects after an abortion. These range from irritability, difficulty sleeping, and depression to post-traumatic stress disorder.

Late-Term Labor Induction

Performed in weeks 22 to 38 of pregnancy. This type of abortion is never performed in a clinic setting, as it may require a hospital stay. Drugs are given to the mother to terminate the pregnancy and to begin labor (usually starts in 2-4 hours). In the event that the placenta is not completely removed during labor, the cervix must be opened, and a doctor will perform suction curettage.

Labor and delivery are remarkably similar to childbirth, with the duration depending upon the size of the unborn child (along with the condition of the uterus). It may be necessary for instruments to be used to scrape the placenta to remove all traces of the unborn child and placenta. The further along in the pregnancy, the greater the chances of the delivered child living. If the baby is removed alive, the doctor is required by law to provide care and treatment to it as they would any other baby born under similar circumstances.

Possible side effects and risks are similar to other procedures, including:

- Pelvic infection (sepsis)
- Incomplete abortion
- Blood clots in the uterus
- Heavy bleeding (hemorrhage)
- Cut or torn cervix
- Perforation of the uterus wall
- Anesthesia-related complications
- Rh immune Globulin Therapy (could endanger future pregnancies)

Long-Term Medical Abortion Risks:

- Future childbearing – in some cases, complications associated with abortion may make it difficult or impossible to become pregnant in the future.

Psychological Abortion Risks:

It is important to note that some women encounter a variety of psychological effects after an abortion. These range from irritability, difficulty sleeping, and depression to post-traumatic stress disorder.

Hysterotomy (Similar To A C-Section)

Performed in weeks 22 to 38 of pregnancy. This type of abortion is never performed in a clinic setting, as it requires a hospital stay. A hysterotomy is performed when a labor induction fails or is not possible. This is the removal of an unborn child by cutting open the abdomen and uterus and terminating the unborn child prior to removal. An anesthetic is given to the woman to remove the pain of surgery.

Possible side effects and risks are similar to other procedures, including:

- Pelvic infection (sepsis)
- Incomplete abortion
- Blood clots in the uterus
- Heavy bleeding (hemorrhage)

- Cut or torn cervix
- Perforation of the uterus wall
- Anesthesia-related complications
- Rh immune Globulin Therapy (could endanger future pregnancies)

Long-Term Medical Abortion Risks:

- Future childbearing – in some cases, complications associated with abortion may make it difficult or impossible to become pregnant in the future.

Psychological Abortion Risks:

It is important to note that some women encounter a variety of psychological effects after an abortion. These range from irritability, difficulty sleeping, and depression to post-traumatic stress disorder.

Pastors of today know that a church without adults has no future; they should preach a sermon on Mother's Day on the types of abortion from this list above and the risks to mothers who sacrificed 1.5 billion children in the last 50 years worldwide!

Pastors chose not to speak on the subject of birth control, knowing that the offering of tithes is not paid by children, dead or alive. However, at the end of the day, men are included in birth control; about 50 million men have had a vasectomy - approximately 5% of all married men of reproductive age. More than 500,000 men elect to have vasectomies every year in the U.S.

Not surprisingly, the age distributions of vasectomy recipients and of men aged 20-74 in the general population were different. Nearly 2/3 (63%) of vasectomy recipients were in their 30's, and only 7% were aged 45-74; but with that understanding, 82,945 men had vasectomies, and Protestants had the highest rate at 8.44 per 1,000 men.

The incidence of vasectomy in the military was 7.10 per 1,000 men, with an age-adjusted rate of 8.66 per 1,000 men; a higher percentage within the military (61%) was performed than reported in the general population. Studies have shown that men who receive vasectomies in the U.S. are typically white, non-Hispanic, and live in the North Central Country; they tend to have private insurance with a price usually about $1,000.

The study also revealed that vasectomy changes a man's personality. Other possible links between vasectomy and a second form of dementia called frontotemporal dementia (FTD) were found. Among 30 men who had undergone a vasectomy, 37 percent had this form of dementia, which causes changes in one's personality, a lack of judgment, and bizarre behavior. Another type of dementia, primary progressive aphasia (PPA), is a neurological disease that causes difficulty with language. Unlike Alzheimer's disease, PPA causes no difficulty with memory but instead features trouble expressing oneself and understanding others.

It is not clear why this link exists, but having a vasectomy raises the risk of semen mixing into the bloodstream. This may trigger an immune response, causing the body to produce warrior cells called antibodies to defend the body against the "foreign" sperm. If these antibodies crossed into the brain, they could cause damage that would result in both forms of dementia. Headaches with vestibular damage can be chronic.

Vasectomy is associated with a statistically significantly increased long-term risk of prostate cancer. Right now, urologists should not tell patients anything based on their findings that the vasectomy causes something that is harmful to the brain. Vasectomy may be a risk factor for primary progressive aphasia; they believe the procedure may induce immune responses to sperm, which shares antigenic epitopes with the brain.

Regarding religious association over birth control and abortion, seven broad categories were created to simplify the data despite over 100 various religious groups being reported. The categories were Catholic, Protestant, other Christian, Muslim, Jewish, no preference, and unknown other; the highest rate was among those describing themselves as Protestants and the lowest as Jewish. Birth control use and abortion are mutilation or a practice of defiling the body and rendering it unfit. Debauchery.

Isaiah chapter 1: 4,5,7,9,15,28,30, The lofty looks of man shall be humbled, and the haughtiness of men shall be bowed down, and the Spirit alone shall be exalted in this day. For the Spirit shall be upon everyone that is proud and lofty, and upon everyone that is lifted up: and he shall be brought low.

Cease ye from man, whose breath is in his nostrils; for wherein is he to be accounted of?

Isaiah chapter 3: 15,16,17,18,19,20,21,22,23,24,25,26,

There Is A Time For Judgment

My spirit was inspired to say this: "Hear ye indeed, but understand not, and see you indeed, but perceive not." Their disobedience makes the heart of this people fat, making their ears heavy, and shutting their eyes; lest they see with their spiritual eyes, and hear with their spiritual ears, and understand with their spiritual heart, and be converted, and be healed, then said I, how long?

Until the cities are wasted without inhabitants, the houses are without men, and the land is utterly desolate, and the men are removed far away, there will be a great forsaking in the midst of the land.

Where are the remnants; who are the ones that refused to be mutilated? Where are the wombs that have been untouched by Molech? A generation of people have not bowed their knees to the world; they have kept their bodies whole (holy) and unblemished, untattooed, unpierced, and undefiled.

It is too late to baby-boom America again; the women

and men have mutilated and destroyed the temple of their own bodies. Every Sunday, the show service must go on; the airwaves with rituals and flattery phrases, praises of chemistry worship among themselves. Only with their lips, for their ears to hear; worldly hearts are far from being spiritually obedient.

There is a time to be born, a time to be a child, a time to be a man to put away all childish things, and the home of a man should be full of his children. Happy is a man whose home is full of the blessings of the spirit; "Children are the blessing of the spirit! A man's inheritance is his children. A woman's blessings are her children!" The only way to be praised into the gates is the song of praises by a mother's children and her husband. Not the choir or the pastor.

Adam was Eve's glory, and their blessing was not a dog, horse to ride upon, or even a house, but their children. A nation is born of a woman as a blessing. America, the United States' wealth is given to the family; every man and woman together is given a household that is full of children, which is their blessing.

America is the land of the oh-so-beautiful, but where are your spiritual blessings?

A man is like a tree, a fig tree, not an apple or orange, but he should bear fruit. A womb is where the fruit is ripened; a womb that is mutilated is worthless and soon withers and dies. The fields are bare; the crop has not been planted for the harvest of the year 2040! How many young people will be 18 years of age then? Not enough, not nearly enough to support a nation! "When he saw a fig tree in the way, he came to it, and found nothing thereon, but leaves only, and said unto it, Let no fruit grow on thee henceforward forever. And presently, the fig tree withered away."

The fig tree that bears no fruit (unfruitful-mutilated-defiled) is broken off and soon cast away into the fire to be burnt; do you now understand the parable of the fig tree? "Verily I say unto you, this generation shall not pass till all these things be fulfilled."

"For as in the days before the flood they were eating and drinking, marrying and giving in marriage, until the day that Noah entered the ark." "Heaven and earth shall pass away, as some may know it to be, but DIVINE WILL shall not pass away."

What must we say about these things? Shall we continue (practicing hatred, birth control, and aborting - robbing the spirit of tithes – killing babies) in sin that grace may abound? Shall you continue to be slaves of sin under the law? Do you not understand to know that to whom you present yourselves slaves to obey, you are that one's slaves who you obey, whether of sin leading to death-hell-and destruction (of the body) or obedience leading to righteousness?

What fruit did you have then in the things you are now ashamed of? The payment of sin is death. Lust of the flesh payments are made by those bound in sin until death seemingly is the only way out; ROE VS. WADE is a tradeoff for hidden sin. Hide your iniquities for the child's life, BUT BE NOT DECEIVED; YOUR SINS SHALL FIND YOU OUT. THERE IS NO HIDING PLACE IN HELL!

You can't bargain with the DIVINE WILL; if you say you have not sinned, you are not only a murderer, but a thief and a liar, and no thief or liar or murderer or they that defiled the body shall be of faith!

I must speak unto you as unto spiritual, but as unto carnal, even as unto babes. You have been fed milk and not with meat, for hitherto ye were not able to bear it, neither yet now are you able. You still walk as a division of men in different forms of bondage called churches of creed, race, and color, but The DIVINE WILL is without those things!

Psalms 118:8 Have we not been told a warning it is best to "follow no man?" Who did Moses lead? A multitude across the dry lands and into the edge of the promised land, where they all perished. Moses did not lead the people where he was not permitted to go himself.

Adam was deceived as much in the same manner as Adam was in the garden; they were only allowed to look but not touch! David was tempted with just a look at Bathsheba on the roof, and Job sinned with his eyelids, too! Moses deserted his wife and sons on the other side of the sea after the waters came crashing down. Zipporah was Moses' wife of living water at the well when he was in bondage, but the rock that he smote was just a rock that gave water in the desert that was as stubborn as the people and Moses, their leader.

Zipporah followed after Moses as long as he allowed her (then he made his own law as men do today), only to travel in the wilderness and still not be allowed to enter the promised land without Zipporah! "What does it profit a man to gain the universe (even a look) and lose his Soul?"

The only adult that has a right to lead anyone is one man: a married man and the father of their children. A female is to obey her parents, and when she is joined to her husband, her one and only husband, she must obey and follow him only. Where did Adam and Eve go? Why do you need to know which is private and none of your business?

They went off by themselves, and no other man ruled Adam's household of faith. If a man (doesn't have faith) can't provide for his own household (himself), he cannot (not fit to) provide for the household (the gift of favor, being a spiritual wife and blessings, being children) of faith.

The just shall live by faith; without faith, your spirit cannot please the DIVINE WILL or even have the truth, which is of the Spirit of Light. If any man defiles the temple of the spirit (your body), he shall the spirit destroy (sickness, diseases, and death) for the temple of the spirit is "Whole, (within)." Which temple are you in? Spirit or that of outer forms? You still bow your knees to worship when the DIVINE WILL within lifts up the bow down your head and keeps even the foot from slipping and the body from being bowed down in distress.

Answer to the DIVINEWILL: for what cause did the 1.5 billion estimated lives of your own children sacrificed? For the love of money - the root of all evil. You seek after the knowledge to support the careers and education of this world, to feed the lusts of your vanities, to put off the births of children to enjoy the sexual pleasures being devoured in your lust.

You just didn't and still don't have the time to be parents of not too many, hardly any children. All that heaven allows was not pertaining to children; eight is too many, and ½ dozen are still too many; 2 or 3 is too soon, and one is aborted, and tonight we savor the seduction of the wealth we have worked so hard for. YE HAVE SOLD YOURSELVES FOR NOTHING!

Those who did have children raised them to be institutionalized in Camps, Schools, Centers, and Childcare Institutions. They learn to read and write and become abandoned by family by joining training classes and anything for their parents to be free of them. How many children have been socially neglected, abused mentally and physically by peer pressure in the process of being dropped off by parents who don't have time for them?

Abortions were done in a society where 70% of Christians eat, drink and are merry, not suffering little children to live, but putting them to death. Your own vain, empty lives did not include a child at the time; drop them off on someone else was like sending them all away behind the closed doors of our amnesiac-amnesia minds and putting them out of sight and out of mind!

Yet for 50 years, you pleasured yourselves, heaping up the treasures of this world, where moths ate, rust corroded, and thieves stole. Even to this day, you are like greedy dogs that can never have enough. Your leaders' watchmen are blind; they are all ignorant; they are all dumb dogs that cannot bark sleeping, lying down, loving to slumber. Yes, they are greedy dogs that can never have enough, and they are shepherds that cannot understand.

They all look their own way, every one for his gain, from his quarter. You say I will fetch wine, and we will fill ourselves with strong drinks, and tomorrow shall be like this day, and much more abundant. Your hands are defiled; your hands have been lifted up in vanities, and your mouths have spoken deceitfully. Your heads are bowed down, and your eyes are still blind because of your iniquities.

Adam and Eve never bowed or prayed; Noah never

prayed; why? Because they had faith that was absent of doubt, fear, and unbelief. They were "proactive"; praying is reactive, asking for help when we should just be still, silent, and know The WILL IS SPIRIT OVER OUR SPIRIT, moving all things; the good, bad, and the ugly, all have a season in time for the purpose of us having our being.

The promise seeds of Abraham have been slain by the multitude of the congregation; 1.5 billion blessed seeds as grains of sand have been scattered in your vanities; your greed has swelled you up in pride before a fall and your haughtiness before destruction. Your sins indeed are as scarlet; how can you sing in a barren land? What land?

The wombs are barren, and this is the time when the estimated 1.5 billion promise seeds would flourish in our nation: building up a strong nation, a healthy nation of prosperity. But, like a wicked woman that tears down her house with her own hands, so have this nation been torn down with the hands of a woman!

Women have labored but not in the home; men have led but not in their homes, with their wives chosen by the spirit. All men have chosen wives of strangeness, unyoked and unjointed by the blindness of the people's law. The law can't give love, and love doesn't give the law; love is the Divine will above the laws of principalities!

Joel 2: Blow ye the trumpet in Zion and sound an alarm in my holy mountain. Let all the inhabitants of the land tremble; Woe the day of the Lord cometh, for it is nigh at hand. A day of darkness and of gloominess, a day of clouds and of thick darkness as the morning spread upon the mountains.

These are the years after many generations; a fire

devoured before them, and behind them, a flame burning the land is like the garden of Eden before them, and behind them, a desolate wilderness...

IF WE COULD TURN BACK THE HANDS OF TIME...

If we could go back 50 years ago, to change the course of time. We would stand up for the right to life, AGAINST ROE VS. WADE, we as a nation would JUST SAY "NO! "The 1.5 estimated billion lives then would all be saved, Not where iniquity of guilt has hidden their grave. But, employed somewhere in the grand old U.S. of A. Okay, say, can you see it by the error of our way? The day is at hand. We had to overturn ROE VS WADE.

50 years have come and passed so swiftly. A dark cloud has rolled overhead since We lost 1.5 billion estimated lives. Our nation is nearly cast away in dollars and cents.

The market stocks are at a crashing rate, and inflation has begun knocking at our front door. An unfamiliar 40-year low Employment rate has knocked us on the floor.

All because of ROE VS WADE. We could have, should have, would have just said "NO! "The day is at hand. We must now do with what we can. Try to birth our nation. From the oh-so-few few left of fertile women and men!

ROE VS. WADE was a dysfunctional, discriminating LAW, exploiting being female, McCorvey made many mistakes, which made her life and ours a living hell. The courts ruled in her favor. A dysfunctional law ruled against the right to life proved to be loveless and against us all.

No weapon formed against us shall prosper, so the Bible

says. And it actually stands true. Where McCorvey's 3 children's lives were saved, while our own 1.5 estimated billion were dismantled and dismayed!

Who can be against us? The Lord God Lucifer didn't forbid our mothers to forsake us; will the Lord God of this world be our trust? Though a host of enemies were encamped as an evil veil, not a hair on Norma's children's head was harmed. Norma's weapon formed against her own children's life failed.

1.5 billion estimated babies died. Tossed by an angry, bloody death wave 3 years, the courts of a nation gruelled, Sparing the life of Norma's 3 children in those days now lives as neither pro-life nor pro-choice today, proving Divine Will Saves!

ROE VS. WADE angered the DIVINE WILL choosing who can or cannot live. Perhaps just one citizen from the womb of one of Norma's daughters speaks up to say. Would have, could have, should have voted for the right to live. But they refused to help overturn ROE VS. WADE!

None in just 1.5 billion estimated aborted are alive today. But 4 out of 5 in the Supreme Court voted and overturned ROE VS. WADE! Never have so few done so much good against one woman who sabotaged the U.S. of A.

A little child shall lead them indeed that's true today. For the prosperity of our nation is in the conception of a child of doom. The heartbeat of a nation is in the conception of the womb.

The prosperity of a nation is in the right to live and not cast away. The right to life and rejoice over the cells of the U.S. of A. By the overturning of ROE VS. WADE!

Baby booming American once more again. Overturned ROE VS. WADE

Birth-right is life to the unborn, birthrights are given by a father and mother's HONORING. Redeeming life of we the people in the womb unblemished by others birthrights of Fathers sowing seeds on fertile wombs of the U. S. of A.

Conceptions of birthrights sown within the wombs of our Dear mothers today, birthrights are why we, the people went back in time, we could have would have should have said no, 50 years ago, ROE VS. WADE, we just OVERTURNED, American people just said "NO!"

"I am the voice in the book"

Statistics

1.5 estimated billion babies were killed by abortions in the U.S. within the last 50 years; Christians did 70 % of these babies' deaths. 62 % of users of sterilization are Christians, 29 % of users of long-acting reversible contraceptives are Christians, and Christians were 48 % of the users of hormonal methods. The bottom line, however, whatever and everything like that, at the end of the day, all religions, evangelical Protestant, Catholic, use the blanket of "reproductive health" services.

In the 1970's and 80's, the Bethesda Home for Girls forced pregnant girls to give up their newborns for adoption to Christian families who paid a $250 "love gift," a former judicial officer recently called the facility a "baby selling factory." Britain's adoption scandal broke the silence and related the stories of several women whose babies were given up for adoption over 30 years ago. Adoption reached a peak in 1968 when more than 16,000 babies born to unmarried mothers were handed over to new families. Catholic church in Australia apologized for the forced adoption of 150,000 babies in Catholic-run hospitals. In Britain, religious institutions ran 150 mother-and-baby homes in the postwar years. Highgate, north London, founded by an order of nuns, organized the adoption of thousands of babies before it closed in 1971.

Young women were obliged to work in the laundry in return for their keep. In 1976, the primary responsibility for handling adoptions was moved from voluntary organizations, mainly religious, to local authorities.

The Catholic Children's Society- called the Crusade of Rescue until 1985 - pointed to different social attitudes in the postwar decades. "When you look back to the 1940's, '50's, and '60's, in society in general and terms of government policy, there was extraordinarily little support for unmarried mothers, or mothers who were married but had a child by a different man, "Society's attitudes have changed.

"From looking back at our records from sample years, we estimate that 75% of mothers that came to our organization kept their babies, but it would have been difficult for them because of the values of wider society.

The Crusade of Rescue had lobbied for a change of law to allow adopted children and birth mothers to discover details about the circumstances of the adoption. Since 1975, adopted children have had the legal right to obtain their birth and adoption records. The Salvation Army was accounted for responding in a television documentary, saying, "We sincerely sympathize with memories and can only confirm that experience would be different today.

However, Christians support each other in their religion; it's a circuit of a continuous cycle of deceiving and being deceived. Even if a Christian gets pregnant and does not abort her baby, she can put her baby up for adoption, and another Christian can adopt her child. But the iniquity is done; this child is still a conception that was denied a right to his own parents. A baby is made an orphan when both parents are deceased or abandon him at the time of his birth or giving and placing him up for adoption.

What does the bible say about such a child? Exodus 22:22 Ye shall not afflict any widow or fatherless child. If thou afflict them in any wise, and they cry at all unto me, I will surely hear their cry, and my wrath shall wax hot.

Let's take a spiritual eye view at the congregation of a Sunday morning worship service; do you see the mark of the beast? It indeed is the number of a man; it is also a mark; it is a blemish, a spot, a wrinkle, and/or that patch on the arm.

A tattoo, a piercing, or even a device placed by your surgeon under the skin for control, your sign of the beast is your own choice of self-mutilation. The patch many Christian women wear on their arms is not a card to get money but a device that keeps them working on their jobs that pay them money!

The sign of the beast is the number of a man, the life of a man, and the day of conception stands for the number of one man; the mark of the beast is the destruction of the body. The mark of the beast is the mutilation of the body; the hallmark of the enemy is to steal, kill, and destroy! He always leaves his mark upon his victims; he has pride in his deception, and his stamp of disapproval is a branding.

Weeping and gnashing of teeth? Many have called Lord, Lord, but are workers of iniquity shall depart...

And the beast which I saw was like unto a leopard

(Christians who are hypocrites, as leopards having spots that can't be changed), and his feet were as the feet of a bear (footprints of a cold-hearted brut-beast). His mouth was the (womb of a woman) the mouth of a lion, and the dragon (men) gave him his power (seeds), his seat (government), and great authority.

And I saw one of his heads as it was wounded to death (women dying from birth control and abortion), and his deadly wound was healed (Sterilization), and all the world wondered after the beast.

And they worshipped (controlled birth) the dragon (the passing of Roe v. Wade!") which gave power (made murder a lawful right) unto the beast: and they worshipped the beast (used birth control), saying, who is like unto the beast? Who can make war with him?

Revelations 13- And there was given unto him a mouth speaking remarkable things and blasphemies (the lawyers that stood for pro-choice). Power was given unto him to continue for forty-two months. (from the filing of Roe v. Wade" to the rights granted into law in 1973)

And he (unholy men) opened his mouth in blasphemy (cursed) against God, to blaspheme his name, and his (churches) tabernacle, (women and men) and (supported birth control and abortion against) them that dwell in heaven. (the unborn in the womb)

And it was given unto him to make (the testing of failure or proving of one's faith) war with the (Christians) saints, and to overcome them: and power (pro-choice) was given him over all kindreds, and tongues, and nations. The mutilation of the temple (body) is an end-time sign of the mark of the beast.

And all (having the mark of the beast) that dwell upon the earth shall worship him, whose names are not written in the book of life of the Lamb slain (aborted) from the foundation (conception of the womb) of the world.

He that have clean heart, and have not lifted up his soul unto vanity, and have not sworn deceitfully...

If any man has an ear, let him hear.

I AM THE VOICE IN THE BOOK

www.ingramcontent.com/pod-product-compliance
Lightning Source LLC
LaVergne TN
LVHW050601160826
845677LV00011B/2415

9798896911906